MAKING BANK

A Money Management Workbook for Erotic Entrepreneurs

By Princess Kali

Published by Erotication Publications
San Jose, CA

Cover design by Hannah Portello-Swagel
Book design by Hannah Portello-Swagel and Kali Williams

ISBN: 978-1-7340461-5-1

Printed in the United States of America

CONTENT

Getting Started

Monthly Budgets

Yearly Wrap-up

Resources + Helpful Info

DISCLAIMER

I'm an **experienced ProDomme, kink educator, and entrepreneur**, and this book is based on what I have learned through many years of personal experience and research. But it is **not intended to provide legal or financial advice**, nor should it be used as such without first consulting with a legal or financial professional to determine **what is best for your individual needs**.

—INTRO

"I love making money, but I hate keeping track of it."

This was my mindset for many, many years. I started my career in sex work as a stripper, and it seemed like there was an endless supply of dollar bills as long as I was willing to get out there and dance for them. And then I became a professional dominatrix. I had a tribute rate of hundreds of dollars an hour, and I received gifts such as Louboutins and international travel on a regular basis. So I never really worried about keeping track of the money I made, because I figured it was always "easy" to go out and make more.

Eventually, I realized that my aversion to tracking my money had a few specific roots.

First, I have dyscalculia, a learning disability related to numbers. My mind finds even the simplest of numbers to be difficult to keep track of, which is both frustrating and (unnecessarily) embarrassing.

Second, the supposed ease of earning more money made money seem almost unreal, like board game money. This is a common feeling among current and former sex workers, and the result is often that the "easy" money slips through our fingers like sand.

Third, I didn't come from a family that talked about money or how to manage it responsibly. We weren't particularly wealthy, but we weren't poor, either. Both of my parents used spending to soothe stress or celebrate special occasions, so I learned to associate spending with pleasure, without understanding how to balance immediate gratification with long-term planning.

All three of these struggles are common for sex workers, and in combination with the appearance of "easy" money, they can result in less-than-ideal financial management practices.

As I've gotten older, my goals around money have changed. While I used to feel successful because I could spend money on impulsive daily desires at any time and had a shoe collection that c-list celebrities would covet, now I have two bigger goals: I want to buy a fabulous house on a large property to satisfy a lifelong desire to own a home of my very own, and I want to ensure I have financial stability for the rest of my life. Slowly, I realized that my money habits (my impulsive spending and my refusal to see money as "real") were getting in the way of my big money goals (long-term stability and large-scale investments), and I knew I had to make a change.

My financial life was transformed when I got help managing my finances and started to rectify past mistakes. I was even more empowered when I started adapting a generic budget workbook to track my money in a way that was more interactive and right for my brain.

When I launched the Red Key Club, a business and marketing school for sex workers, I included a series of discussions on money management. During those discussions, we talked about the difficulties in tracking money and the unique challenges that sex workers face around financial planning. I was a bit surprised to find that so many folks prefer analog tracking, just like me. But I was excited to discover that shared preference with so many people in my network, because it meant I knew I could help. Those conversations are what inspired me to create this workbook, and my hope is that it helps you up your money management game.

Good luck—you've got this!

Kali

—TIPS FOR USING THIS WORKBOOK

- You can track your numbers daily, weekly, or monthly. **The most important thing is that you track them!**

- **Schedule time in your calendar for budgeting and looking at your money.** Don't just assume you'll do it. Instead, get yourself into the habit by putting it on your to-do list and holding yourself accountable for getting it done.

- If you can't track things immediately, be sure to **keep receipts or notes** to make sure you can track them later. It can be frustrating to have to go back and track down the numbers to put in the workbook. **Create a place where you automatically put your receipts** (a basket by the door, an envelope at your desk, etc.) to keep them organized for when you need them.

- If it's helpful, feel free to use colored pens, stickers, or anything else you need to make things **visual and fun** so you'll be consistent.

- **Everything is more fun with a friend.** Pick an accountability partner, and set up a regular check-in to talk about your numbers or spend an hour catching up on your bookkeeping together (remotely or in the same place) and then chatting about what you learned about your budget and money management.

- That being said, **make sure you pick the right friend**! Money is a touchy subject, and you don't want jealousy, insecurity, or cattiness undermining your hard work and success.

- **Rewards work!** Pick out a reward that's tailored to your goals, and treat yourself when you reach a milestone. (Just be sure the reward fits into your budget! It defeats the purpose if it turns into backsliding. Free rewards are great too, such as relaxing with a book you've been meaning to read, making art, or cooking your favorite meal.)

- **Keep an open mind.** This workbook might be just one step on your journey to figuring out your best system, or it might be a perfect fit. But I promise there is no "one true way" of managing your money.

- It helps a lot to **set up automatic payment for bills** that are the same each month. Keep enough money available to pay each bill without overdrafting your bank account or busting your credit limit, then turn on auto pay so you have one less thing to worry about.

TIPS FOR USING THIS WORKBOOK

- If you have a bank account, you should **sign up for an online account** and check every few days to keep an eye out for fraudulent or duplicate charges and to make sure that the numbers in your account match the numbers in your mind (and your workbook).

- **Some expenses can be averaged** to better budget for them in the future (such as food or transportation), and **other expenses may fluctuate** with the seasons (such as using more energy for heat or A/C during peak months).

- Remember that **income can also fluctuate due to external factors** (such as industry or economy trends) or internal factors (such as needing to take a health break or being distracted by other needs in your life).

- Last but not least, **be forgiving and compassionate with yourself**. Learning to budget is like building any other habit. Just because you skip a day (or a month), it doesn't mean you've messed it up completely. You can always pick it back up again, but the sooner you do, the better off you'll be. **Start wherever you are, and go from there.**

YEAR:

PRE-PLANNING REFLECTIONS

Historically, what are your struggles around money?

Examples:

- Compulsive spending
- Spending more than you make
- Being afraid to spend any money at all
- Accumulating too much debt
- Not having any savings or an emergency fund
- Not having a budget or money management skills
- Not feeling comfortable talking about money
- Feeling overwhelmed at managing your finances

PRE-PLANNING REFLECTIONS

How are you going to overcome them this year?

PRE-PLANNING REFLECTIONS

What are your general financial goals for the next year?

—PRE-PLANNING REFLECTIONS

What resources are you going to use to reach your goals?

SHIFTING YOUR MINDSET

While mindset isn't everything, it can make a huge impact, not just on your earning potential but also on the way it feels to keep track of your money. Let go of old, negative mindsets, and **shift your thinking using positive, optimistic language.**

Old Mindset	New Mindset
I'm only worth as much as my time costs.	I'm valuable regardless of my productivity.
I'm not good at keeping track of money.	I'm improving my understanding of money.
I can spend as much as I want.	I enjoy saving money for the future.
I can't spend any money this month.	I can live well while spending responsibly.
I'll always be as broke as I am now.	I'm building my wealth one day at a time.
I'll manage my money when there's more of it.	I'm laying a foundation for future wealth.

SHIFTING YOUR MINDSET

Old Mindset	→	New Mindset

MOTTOS, GOALS, AND INTENTIONS

Let's break down **what these three things are** and **how you're going to use them** in this workbook.

Motto

A motto is a short phrase (also sometimes called a mantra) that encapsulates a belief or ideal. This can be used to **shift and focus your thinking** to retrain your brain toward **new, more positive thoughts and habits**. You can and should say these out loud to yourself to reinforce the belief.

Examples:

- I'm in control of my money.
- I'm open to abundance in all forms.
- My customers joyfully pay my full rate,

Goal

A goal is a specific objective that you commit to achieving. Goals are different from dreams because they are **measurable**. This allows you to **make clear plans** and keep track of how close you are to achieving them.

Examples:

- Have $1,000 in savings for an emergency fund
- Buy a car
- Pay off debt

Intention

An intention is a small daily habit you commit to building that will help you **live out your mottos** and achieve your goals. These small actions or thought exercises help you **align your everyday actions with your vision for yourself.**

Examples:

- I will be mindful in how I spend my money.
- I will use and wear what I already have.
- I will subscribe to money management newsletters/podcasts.

EXAMPLES OF INCOME STREAMS

An income stream is a way to make money. **Circle or highlight** the income streams you'll be focusing on this year. Use the notes section to **brainstorm more ideas or details.**

Sessions

- In-person
- Phone
- Cam
- Email
- Text

Online Content

- Membership site
- Photo sets
- Custom video clips
- Custom audio clips

Writing

- Guest articles
- Self-published books
- Traditional publishing

Other

- Monetary gifts
- Sales of personal items

Notes:

EXAMPLES OF COSTS/EXPENSES

Circle or highlight the costs/expenses you're expecting this year. Use the notes section to brainstorm more ideas or details.

Business

- Taxes (federal/state income and sales)
- Bookkeeping
- Corporation fees
- Marketing/advertising
- Website hosting and development
- Software such as video or photo editing
- Photography
- Tech such as webcams, phones, laptops, cameras, lights
- Travel (professional)
- Playspace/dungeon (your own space and/or rentals)
- Continuing education such as books, subscriptions, classes, and coaching
- Mailbox, mailing materials, and postage

Life

- Rent/mortgage
- Utilities (power, internet, cable, water, sewage, trash)
- Home maintenance (lawn/landscaping, repairs)
- Insurances (car, rental, health, dental)
- Car (payment, gas, maintenance)
- Other transportation (bus, train, Uber/Lyft)
- Entertainment (movies, music, books, streaming services, TV)
- Food (groceries, restaurants)
- Health (therapy, insurance copays, out of pocket payments, medication, dental)
- Travel (personal)
- Clothes (personal)
- Childcare
- Pets (food, treats, toys, vet bills, medicine, grooming, poop bags/kitty litter)
- Charity
- Spending cash/impulse shopping
- Gifts

Appearance

- Hair
- Makeup
- Nails
- Tanning
- Waxing
- Skin care
- Gym/Yoga

Sex + Kink

- Clothes
- Costumes
- Shoes
- Props
- Toys
- Equipment

Long-term

- Debt payments such as credit cards or student loans
- Savings (e.g., money markets, CDs)
- Retirement (e.g., traditional IRA, Roth IRA)
- School
- Real Estate
- Investing (e.g., mutual funds)

Notes:

TAXES

Paying taxes is a critical part of creating a stable financial life. You'll make it a lot easier on yourself if you **prepare ahead of time** to pay them rather than scrambling at the last minute.

These pages are a place for you to **keep track of all the tax rates and amounts of money you'll need to save**. It's best to find your exact tax number so you're working with accurate information, but a good rule of thumb is 30% of your targeted total (gross) income. That means that **approximately 30 cents out of every dollar you make needs to be put away for tax purposes.**

At the end of the calendar year, you'll receive a variety of IRS forms documenting your income:

- **1099**: Typical independent contractor form that a company that is paying you has filed with the IRS that shows what they paid you (gross wages).

- **W2**: A form an employer files if they have deemed you a full-time employee as opposed to a contractor. This will show the taxes that have been filed on your behalf.

All of this is relevant to how and when you file your taxes. If you receive only 1099s, it's likely that no federal or state tax has been paid on your behalf. That means that the total amount due is the total amount you need to pay (after appropriate expenses have been deducted).

Again, if it feels too complicated to do this yourself, talk to a tax professional. H&R Block is reputed to be sex worker friendly, but that may change from place to place, so do your research.

Do you have 1099 or w2 forms coming from anyone? Write them down.

STATE TAXES

Some states have no state income tax, some have flat state income tax (regardless of income level), and some have graduated percentages based on how much you make.

To find your exact state income tax, Google **[insert name of state] income tax rates**.

You can also check out this Wikipedia page, which is informative but subject to change. **bit.ly/StateTaxInfo**

Calculate Your State Taxes

	x	$	=	$
Your State Income Tax Rate (e.g 0.12 for 12%)		**Your Total Income**		**State Tax Amount Due**

When To Use These Formulas

You'll use the formulas on these two pages to **calculate income tax for each quarter (federal), or each year (state).**

In the **yearly wrap-up section** at the end of this workbook, there's a place for you to **calculate your after-tax income** so you can see how much money you'll have after taxes.

You can **do this at the beginning of the year** as you make a budget based on your projected income and then again **at the end of the year** based on what you actually earn.

FEDERAL TAXES

How to file electronically: **bit.ly/FileIRS**

Check **IRS.gov**, and search for **f1040es** to find quarterly payment dates.

These payments are **due four times per year**, and they're **based on your projected annual income**. (For example, if you make $25,000 in the first quarter, then your payment amount will be based on the prediction that you'll earn $100,000 for the year.) When you calculate your annual taxes **in April, you'll either pay a little more or be eligible for a refund** based on how your actual income compares to your estimates.

You'll be paying into two "buckets" with your quarterly/annual federal taxes:

- **Social security** (includes Medicare): 15.3% of gross income
- **Federal tax**: typically 10-12% of gross income

Here are **two formulas** to help you calculate **how much to pay each quarter**:

Calculate Social Security Tax

$	x	0.153	=	$
25% of Your Estimated Gross Annual Income		**Social Security (15.3%)**		**Social Security Tax Due**

Calculate Federal Income Tax

$	x	0.12	=	$
25% of Your Estimated Gross Annual Income		**Federal Income Tax (typically 10 - 12%)**		**Federal Income Tax Due**

Reminders:

- If your income is strictly W2, you will only need to file annually.
- Even if you file in all four quarters of the year, you have to file again annually every April.

DOS AND DON'TS FOR SETTING GOALS

- **Don't** set goals based on what you "think" you should be doing.
- **Do** figure out why you are working toward your particular goals.

- **Don't** set so many goals that it's difficult to make any progress.
- **Do** prioritize your goals and track your success.

- **Don't** be vague in the wording of your goals.
- **Do** be specific about what you want to achieve.

- **Don't** leave your timelines for your goals open-ended.
- **Do** motivate yourself with (reasonable) deadlines for goals and milestones.

- **Don't** set a huge goal if you're just starting to up your money management game.
- **Do** remember that small steps will get you there and mini successes will keep you motivated.

- **Don't** try to do everything at once.
- **Do** set one big goal per quarter (three-month time period).

- **Don't** think that you're automatically supposed to know this stuff.
- **Do** find accessible ways to develop your financial literacy (like using this workbook!).

- **Don't** feel like you have to achieve your goals all by yourself.
- **Do** ask your friends what's worked for them or, if you can, hire a financial advisor to help you get on the right track.

- **Don't** think that setting financial goals is a one-and-done sort of thing.
- **Do** create visuals and frequent reminders of your goals to help keep you motivated.

DOS AND DON'TS FOR SETTING GOALS

- **Don't** get too hung up on things you can't control, like the economy at large.
- **Do** stay focused on what you can affect, like sticking to your budget.

- **Don't** be afraid to be flexible when your life circumstances—employment, health, relationships, etc.—change.
- **Do** adjust your goals as needed to reflect your current situation.

- **Don't** beat yourself up for any setbacks.
- **Do** approach each day as a new opportunity to make progress toward your goals.

- **Don't** overlook your progress.
- **Do** celebrate milestones and achievements. Acknowledging wins will help you stay motivated to keep going.

- **Don't** focus on daily earnings as a reflection of how your business is doing. Look at how you're doing quarterly or yearly.
- **Do** remember that your earnings are not a reflection of your self-worth.

- **Don't** think small when it comes to your income.
- **Do** dream big about the kind of money you can earn. You can't earn it if you can't imagine it.

FINANCIAL GOAL

Goal:

Deadline/Timeline:

Specific Steps:

- [ ]
- [ ]
- [ ]
- [ ]
- [ ]

Do I need help from anyone?

How important is this?

Notes:

FINANCIAL GOAL

Goal:

Deadline/Timeline:

Specific Steps:

Do I need help from anyone?

How important is this?

Notes:

FINANCIAL GOAL

Goal:

Deadline/Timeline:

Specific Steps:

Do I need help from anyone?

How important is this?

Notes:

FINANCIAL GOAL

Goal:

Deadline/Timeline:

Specific Steps:

Do I need help from anyone?

How important is this?

Notes:

— FINANCIAL GOAL

Goal:

Deadline/Timeline:

Specific Steps:

- [ ]
- [ ]
- [ ]
- [ ]
- [ ]

Do I need help from anyone?

How important is this?

Notes:

REVENUE GOALS

My total revenue goal this year is ____________

Income Stream	Avg Price	Per Month	Per Year

Total: ____________

YOU'VE GOT THIS!

DEBT TRACKER

Account:		Limit:	
Starting Balance:		Interest Rate:	
Goal Payoff Date:		Min. Payment:	

Due Date	Expected Payment	Actual Payment	Remaining Balance	Notes

DEBT TRACKER

Account:		Limit:	
Starting Balance:		Interest Rate:	
Goal Payoff Date:		Min. Payment:	

Due Date	Expected Payment	Actual Payment	Remaining Balance	Notes

DEBT TRACKER

Account:		Limit:	
Starting Balance:		Interest Rate:	
Goal Payoff Date:		Min. Payment:	

Due Date	Expected Payment	Actual Payment	Remaining Balance	Notes

—GIFT TRACKER

Gift	Giver	Value	Notes

GIFT TRACKER

Gift	Giver	Value	Notes

GIFT TRACKER

Gift	Giver	Value	Notes

TIPS FOR USING THE MONTHLY TRACKERS

- **Don't be afraid of the monthly tracker!** Hiding from the problem won't make it better. You're being brave for facing it, and **you can handle this like the badass you are.**
- The most important thing is that you **use this in whatever way** you're actually going to use it.
- **Use whiteout or cross things out** if they aren't relevant for you.
- If you struggle to differentiate between numbers, **different colored pens can be really helpful**. Red for expenses and green for income, for example.
- Use stickers, doodle, draw, write quotes, add extra mottos—whatever it takes to **make this book feel like your own.**
- If you're getting overwhelmed with tracking everything, **pick one or two things to focus on** and add more as you get comfortable.
- You can record things down to the penny or round up/down to the nearest dollar. Just **be consistent with whatever system you use**.
- **Remember, don't set too many goals all at once!** Set one or two larger goals, and break those down into smaller steps. Make those steps mini-goals to get you to a larger goal.
- **Designate time**, whether it's once a week, once every two weeks, or once a month, to sit down with this workbook, update the trackers, and check your progress toward goals. **Treat that time as an appointment with yourself**, and prioritize it just like you would an appointment with a client.
- If you're having trouble getting excited about spending time with this workbook, **consider stacking it with an activity you enjoy**: treat yourself to a favorite snack while you work, watch a favorite TV show when you're finished, etc.

Want to see examples of filled out trackers?

Check out **MakingBankWorkbook.com/TrackerExamples**

MONTHLY TRACKERS

MONTHLY MOTTO, GOALS, TASKS, INTENTIONS

Month: | | Year: | |

This month's money motto:

Financial Goals:

Financial Tasks:

Intention Setting:

EXPENSE TRACKER

Date	Description	Amount	[Debit, Credit, Cash, Auto Pay]	Category

EXPENSE TRACKER

Date	Description	Amount	[Debit, Credit, Cash, Auto Pay]	Category

EXPENSE TRACKER

Date	Description	Amount	[Debit, Credit, Cash, Auto Pay]	Category

—EXPENSE TRACKER

Date	Description	Amount	[Debit, Credit, Cash, Auto Pay]	Category

INCOME TRACKER

Date	Description	Amount	Notes

INCOME TRACKER

Date	Description	Amount	Notes

INCOME TRACKER

Date	Description	Amount	Notes

INCOME TRACKER

Date	Description	Amount	Notes

MONTHLY SUMMARY - PERSONAL EXPENSES

Category	Expected	Actual	Difference [+/-]	Notes
Tax Reserve				
Rent				
Utilities				
Transportation				
Food				
Entertainment				
Health				
Total:				

MONTHLY SUMMARY - BUSINESS EXPENSES

Category	Expected	Actual	Difference [+/-]	Notes
Tax Reserve				
Marketing/Ads				
Education				
Total:				

MONTHLY SUMMARY - INCOME

Income Source	Expected	Actual	Difference [+/-]	Notes
Total:				

MONTHLY REFLECTIONS

Total Income:

Total Expenses:

Difference:

What did I do well this month?

What did I struggle with this month?

How can I improve next month?

NOTES

MONTHLY MOTTO, GOALS, TASKS, INTENTIONS

Month: ______ Year: ______

This month's money motto:

Financial Goals:

- [ ]
- [ ]
- [ ]

Financial Tasks:

- [ ]
- [ ]
- [ ]

Intention Setting:

EXPENSE TRACKER

Date	Description	Amount	[Debit, Credit, Cash, Auto Pay]	Category

EXPENSE TRACKER

Date	Description	Amount	[Debit, Credit, Cash, Auto Pay]	Category

EXPENSE TRACKER

Date	Description	Amount	[Debit, Credit, Cash, Auto Pay]	Category

EXPENSE TRACKER

Date	Description	Amount	[Debit, Credit, Cash, Auto Pay]	Category

INCOME TRACKER

Date	Description	Amount	Notes

INCOME TRACKER

Date	Description	Amount	Notes

INCOME TRACKER

Date	Description	Amount	Notes

INCOME TRACKER

Date	Description	Amount	Notes

MONTHLY SUMMARY - PERSONAL EXPENSES

Category	Expected	Actual	Difference [+/-]	Notes
Tax Reserve				
Rent				
Utilities				
Transportation				
Food				
Entertainment				
Health				
Total:				

MONTHLY SUMMARY - BUSINESS EXPENSES

Category	Expected	Actual	Difference [+/-]	Notes
Tax Reserve				
Marketing/Ads				
Education				
Total:				

MONTHLY SUMMARY - INCOME

Income Source	Expected	Actual	Difference [+/-]	Notes
Total:				

MONTHLY REFLECTIONS

Total Income:

Total Expenses:

Difference:

What did I do well this month?

What did I struggle with this month?

How can I improve next month?

NOTES

MONTHLY MOTTO, GOALS, TASKS, INTENTIONS

Month: [ ] Year: [ ]

This month's money motto:

Financial Goals:

- [ ]
- [ ]
- [ ]

Financial Tasks:

- [ ]
- [ ]
- [ ]

Intention Setting:

EXPENSE TRACKER

Date	Description	Amount	[Debit, Credit, Cash, Auto Pay]	Category

EXPENSE TRACKER

Date	Description	Amount	[Debit, Credit, Cash, Auto Pay]	Category

EXPENSE TRACKER

Date	Description	Amount	[Debit, Credit, Cash, Auto Pay]	Category

EXPENSE TRACKER

Date	Description	Amount	[Debit, Credit, Cash, Auto Pay]	Category

INCOME TRACKER

Date	Description	Amount	Notes

INCOME TRACKER

Date	Description	Amount	Notes

INCOME TRACKER

Date	Description	Amount	Notes

INCOME TRACKER

Date	Description	Amount	Notes

MONTHLY SUMMARY - PERSONAL EXPENSES

Category	Expected	Actual	Difference [+/-]	Notes
Tax Reserve				
Rent				
Utilities				
Transportation				
Food				
Entertainment				
Health				
Total:				

MONTHLY SUMMARY - BUSINESS EXPENSES

Category	Expected	Actual	Difference [+/-]	Notes
Tax Reserve				
Marketing/Ads				
Education				
Total:				

MONTHLY SUMMARY - INCOME

Income Source	Expected	Actual	Difference [+/-]	Notes
Total:				

MONTHLY REFLECTIONS

Total Income:	
Total Expenses:	
Difference:	

What did I do well this month?

What did I struggle with this month?

How can I improve next month?

NOTES

MONTHLY MOTTO, GOALS, TASKS, INTENTIONS

Month: Year:

This month's money motto:

Financial Goals:

Financial Tasks:

Intention Setting:

EXPENSE TRACKER

Date	Description	Amount	[Debit, Credit, Cash, Auto Pay]	Category

EXPENSE TRACKER

Date	Description	Amount	[Debit, Credit, Cash, Auto Pay]	Category

EXPENSE TRACKER

Date	Description	Amount	[Debit, Credit, Cash, Auto Pay]	Category

—EXPENSE TRACKER

Date	Description	Amount	[Debit, Credit, Cash, Auto Pay]	Category

INCOME TRACKER

Date	Description	Amount	Notes

INCOME TRACKER

Date	Description	Amount	Notes

INCOME TRACKER

Date	Description	Amount	Notes

INCOME TRACKER

Date	Description	Amount	Notes

MONTHLY SUMMARY - PERSONAL EXPENSES

Category	Expected	Actual	Difference [+/-]	Notes
Tax Reserve				
Rent				
Utilities				
Transportation				
Food				
Entertainment				
Health				
Total:				

MONTHLY SUMMARY - BUSINESS EXPENSES

Category	Expected	Actual	Difference [+/-]	Notes
Tax Reserve				
Marketing/Ads				
Education				
Total:				

MONTHLY SUMMARY - INCOME

Income Source	Expected	Actual	Difference [+/-]	Notes
Total:				

MONTHLY REFLECTIONS

Total Income:

Total Expenses:

Difference:

What did I do well this month?

What did I struggle with this month?

How can I improve next month?

NOTES

MONTHLY MOTTO, GOALS, TASKS, INTENTIONS

Month: ______ **Year:** ______

This month's money motto:

Financial Goals:

- [ ]
- [ ]
- [ ]

Financial Tasks:

- [ ]
- [ ]
- [ ]

Intention Setting:

EXPENSE TRACKER

Date	Description	Amount	[Debit, Credit, Cash, Auto Pay]	Category

EXPENSE TRACKER

Date	Description	Amount	[Debit, Credit, Cash, Auto Pay]	Category

EXPENSE TRACKER

Date	Description	Amount	[Debit, Credit, Cash, Auto Pay]	Category

—EXPENSE TRACKER

Date	Description	Amount	[Debit, Credit, Cash, Auto Pay]	Category

INCOME TRACKER

Date	Description	Amount	Notes

INCOME TRACKER

Date	Description	Amount	Notes

INCOME TRACKER

Date	Description	Amount	Notes

INCOME TRACKER

Date	Description	Amount	Notes

MONTHLY SUMMARY - PERSONAL EXPENSES

Category	Expected	Actual	Difference [+/-]	Notes
Tax Reserve				
Rent				
Utilities				
Transportation				
Food				
Entertainment				
Health				
Total:				

MONTHLY SUMMARY - BUSINESS EXPENSES

Category	Expected	Actual	Difference [+/-]	Notes
Tax Reserve				
Marketing/Ads				
Education				
Total:				

MONTHLY SUMMARY - INCOME

Income Source	Expected	Actual	Difference [+/-]	Notes
Total:				

MONTHLY REFLECTIONS

Total Income:

Total Expenses:

Difference:

What did I do well this month?

What did I struggle with this month?

How can I improve next month?

NOTES

MONTHLY MOTTO, GOALS, TASKS, INTENTIONS

Month: ______ Year: ______

This month's money motto:

Financial Goals:

- [ ]
- [ ]
- [ ]

Financial Tasks:

- [ ]
- [ ]
- [ ]

Intention Setting:

EXPENSE TRACKER

Date	Description	Amount	[Debit, Credit, Cash, Auto Pay]	Category

EXPENSE TRACKER

Date	Description	Amount	[Debit, Credit, Cash, Auto Pay]	Category

EXPENSE TRACKER

Date	Description	Amount	[Debit, Credit, Cash, Auto Pay]	Category

EXPENSE TRACKER

Date	Description	Amount	[Debit, Credit, Cash, Auto Pay]	Category

INCOME TRACKER

Date	Description	Amount	Notes

INCOME TRACKER

Date	Description	Amount	Notes

INCOME TRACKER

Date	Description	Amount	Notes

INCOME TRACKER

Date	Description	Amount	Notes

MONTHLY SUMMARY - PERSONAL EXPENSES

Category	Expected	Actual	Difference [+/-]	Notes
Tax Reserve				
Rent				
Utilities				
Transportation				
Food				
Entertainment				
Health				
Total:				

MONTHLY SUMMARY - BUSINESS EXPENSES

Category	Expected	Actual	Difference [+/-]	Notes
Tax Reserve				
Marketing/Ads				
Education				
Total:				

MONTHLY SUMMARY - INCOME

Income Source	Expected	Actual	Difference [+/-]	Notes
Total:				

MONTHLY REFLECTIONS

Total Income:

Total Expenses:

Difference:

What did I do well this month?

What did I struggle with this month?

How can I improve next month?

NOTES

MONTHLY MOTTO, GOALS, TASKS, INTENTIONS

Month: | Year:

This month's money motto:

Financial Goals:

Financial Tasks:

Intention Setting:

EXPENSE TRACKER

Date	Description	Amount	[Debit, Credit, Cash, Auto Pay]	Category

—EXPENSE TRACKER

Date	Description	Amount	[Debit, Credit, Cash, Auto Pay]	Category

EXPENSE TRACKER

Date	Description	Amount	[Debit, Credit, Cash, Auto Pay]	Category

EXPENSE TRACKER

Date	Description	Amount	[Debit, Credit, Cash, Auto Pay]	Category

INCOME TRACKER

Date	Description	Amount	Notes

INCOME TRACKER

Date	Description	Amount	Notes

INCOME TRACKER

Date	Description	Amount	Notes

INCOME TRACKER

Date	Description	Amount	Notes

MONTHLY SUMMARY - PERSONAL EXPENSES

Category	Expected	Actual	Difference [+/-]	Notes
Tax Reserve				
Rent				
Utilities				
Transportation				
Food				
Entertainment				
Health				
Total:				

MONTHLY SUMMARY - BUSINESS EXPENSES

Category	Expected	Actual	Difference [+/-]	Notes
Tax Reserve				
Marketing/Ads				
Education				
Total:				

MONTHLY SUMMARY - INCOME

Income Source	Expected	Actual	Difference [+/-]	Notes
Total:				

—MONTHLY REFLECTIONS

Total Income:

Total Expenses:

Difference:

What did I do well this month?

What did I struggle with this month?

How can I improve next month?

NOTES

MONTHLY MOTTO, GOALS, TASKS, INTENTIONS

Month: 　　　　Year:

This month's money motto:

Financial Goals:

- [ ]
- [ ]
- [ ]

Financial Tasks:

- [ ]
- [ ]
- [ ]

Intention Setting:

EXPENSE TRACKER

Date	Description	Amount	[Debit, Credit, Cash, Auto Pay]	Category

—EXPENSE TRACKER

Date	Description	Amount	[Debit, Credit, Cash, Auto Pay]	Category

EXPENSE TRACKER

Date	Description	Amount	[Debit, Credit, Cash, Auto Pay]	Category

—EXPENSE TRACKER

Date	Description	Amount	[Debit, Credit, Cash, Auto Pay]	Category

INCOME TRACKER

Date	Description	Amount	Notes

—INCOME TRACKER

Date	Description	Amount	Notes

INCOME TRACKER

Date	Description	Amount	Notes

INCOME TRACKER

Date	Description	Amount	Notes

MONTHLY SUMMARY - PERSONAL EXPENSES

Category	Expected	Actual	Difference [+/-]	Notes
Tax Reserve				
Rent				
Utilities				
Transportation				
Food				
Entertainment				
Health				
Total:				

MONTHLY SUMMARY - BUSINESS EXPENSES

Category	Expected	Actual	Difference [+/-]	Notes
Tax Reserve				
Marketing/Ads				
Education				
Total:				

MONTHLY SUMMARY - INCOME

Income Source	Expected	Actual	Difference [+/-]	Notes
Total:				

MONTHLY REFLECTIONS

Total Income:

Total Expenses:

Difference:

What did I do well this month?

What did I struggle with this month?

How can I improve next month?

NOTES

MONTHLY MOTTO, GOALS, TASKS, INTENTIONS

Month: ____________ **Year:** ____________

This month's money motto:

Financial Goals:

- [ ]
- [ ]
- [ ]

Financial Tasks:

- [ ]
- [ ]
- [ ]

Intention Setting:

EXPENSE TRACKER

Date	Description	Amount	[Debit, Credit, Cash, Auto Pay]	Category

EXPENSE TRACKER

Date	Description	Amount	[Debit, Credit, Cash, Auto Pay]	Category

EXPENSE TRACKER

Date	Description	Amount	[Debit, Credit, Cash, Auto Pay]	Category

—EXPENSE TRACKER

Date	Description	Amount	[Debit, Credit, Cash, Auto Pay]	Category

INCOME TRACKER

Date	Description	Amount	Notes

—INCOME TRACKER

Date	Description	Amount	Notes

INCOME TRACKER

Date	Description	Amount	Notes

INCOME TRACKER

Date	Description	Amount	Notes

MONTHLY SUMMARY - PERSONAL EXPENSES

Category	Expected	Actual	Difference [+/-]	Notes
Tax Reserve				
Rent				
Utilities				
Transportation				
Food				
Entertainment				
Health				
Total:				

MONTHLY SUMMARY - BUSINESS EXPENSES

Category	Expected	Actual	Difference [+/-]	Notes
Tax Reserve				
Marketing/Ads				
Education				
Total:				

MONTHLY SUMMARY - INCOME

Income Source	Expected	Actual	Difference [+/-]	Notes
Total:				

MONTHLY REFLECTIONS

Total Income:

Total Expenses:

Difference:

What did I do well this month?

What did I struggle with this month?

How can I improve next month?

NOTES

MONTHLY MOTTO, GOALS, TASKS, INTENTIONS

Month: 　　　　**Year:**

This month's money motto:

Financial Goals:

- [ ]
- [ ]
- [ ]

Financial Tasks:

- [ ]
- [ ]
- [ ]

Intention Setting:

EXPENSE TRACKER

Date	Description	Amount	[Debit, Credit, Cash, Auto Pay]	Category

EXPENSE TRACKER

Date	Description	Amount	[Debit, Credit, Cash, Auto Pay]	Category

EXPENSE TRACKER

Date	Description	Amount	[Debit, Credit, Cash, Auto Pay]	Category

—EXPENSE TRACKER

Date	Description	Amount	[Debit, Credit, Cash, Auto Pay]	Category

INCOME TRACKER

Date	Description	Amount	Notes

INCOME TRACKER

Date	Description	Amount	Notes

INCOME TRACKER

Date	Description	Amount	Notes

INCOME TRACKER

Date	Description	Amount	Notes

MONTHLY SUMMARY - PERSONAL EXPENSES

Category	Expected	Actual	Difference [+/-]	Notes
Tax Reserve				
Rent				
Utilities				
Transportation				
Food				
Entertainment				
Health				
Total:				

MONTHLY SUMMARY - BUSINESS EXPENSES

Category	Expected	Actual	Difference [+/-]	Notes
Tax Reserve				
Marketing/Ads				
Education				
Total:				

MONTHLY SUMMARY - INCOME

Income Source	Expected	Actual	Difference [+/-]	Notes
Total:				

MONTHLY REFLECTIONS

Total Income:

Total Expenses:

Difference:

What did I do well this month?

What did I struggle with this month?

How can I improve next month?

NOTES

MONTHLY MOTTO, GOALS, TASKS, INTENTIONS

Month: ______ **Year:** ______

This month's money motto:

Financial Goals:

- [ ]
- [ ]
- [ ]

Financial Tasks:

- [ ]
- [ ]
- [ ]

Intention Setting:

EXPENSE TRACKER

Date	Description	Amount	[Debit, Credit, Cash, Auto Pay]	Category

EXPENSE TRACKER

Date	Description	Amount	[Debit, Credit, Cash, Auto Pay]	Category

EXPENSE TRACKER

Date	Description	Amount	[Debit, Credit, Cash, Auto Pay]	Category

—EXPENSE TRACKER

Date	Description	Amount	[Debit, Credit, Cash, Auto Pay]	Category

INCOME TRACKER

Date	Description	Amount	Notes

INCOME TRACKER

Date	Description	Amount	Notes

INCOME TRACKER

Date	Description	Amount	Notes

INCOME TRACKER

Date	Description	Amount	Notes

MONTHLY SUMMARY - PERSONAL EXPENSES

Category	Expected	Actual	Difference [+/-]	Notes
Tax Reserve				
Rent				
Utilities				
Transportation				
Food				
Entertainment				
Health				
Total:				

MONTHLY SUMMARY - BUSINESS EXPENSES

Category	Expected	Actual	Difference [+/-]	Notes
Tax Reserve				
Marketing/Ads				
Education				
Total:				

MONTHLY SUMMARY - INCOME

Income Source	Expected	Actual	Difference [+/-]	Notes
Total:				

MONTHLY REFLECTIONS

Total Income:

Total Expenses:

Difference:

What did I do well this month?

What did I struggle with this month?

How can I improve next month?

NOTES

MONTHLY MOTTO, GOALS, TASKS, INTENTIONS

Month: ____________ Year: ____________

This month's money motto:

Financial Goals:

- [ ]
- [ ]
- [ ]

Financial Tasks:

- [ ]
- [ ]
- [ ]

Intention Setting:

EXPENSE TRACKER

Date	Description	Amount	[Debit, Credit, Cash, Auto Pay]	Category

EXPENSE TRACKER

Date	Description	Amount	[Debit, Credit, Cash, Auto Pay]	Category

EXPENSE TRACKER

Date	Description	Amount	[Debit, Credit, Cash, Auto Pay]	Category

EXPENSE TRACKER

Date	Description	Amount	[Debit, Credit, Cash, Auto Pay]	Category

INCOME TRACKER

Date	Description	Amount	Notes

INCOME TRACKER

Date	Description	Amount	Notes

INCOME TRACKER

Date	Description	Amount	Notes

—INCOME TRACKER

Date	Description	Amount	Notes

MONTHLY SUMMARY - PERSONAL EXPENSES

Category	Expected	Actual	Difference [+/-]	Notes
Tax Reserve				
Rent				
Utilities				
Transportation				
Food				
Entertainment				
Health				
Total:				

MONTHLY SUMMARY - BUSINESS EXPENSES

Category	Expected	Actual	Difference [+/-]	Notes
Tax Reserve				
Marketing/Ads				
Education				
Total:				

MONTHLY SUMMARY - INCOME

Income Source	Expected	Actual	Difference [+/-]	Notes
Total:				

MONTHLY REFLECTIONS

Total Income:

Total Expenses:

Difference:

What did I do well this month?

What did I struggle with this month?

How can I improve next month?

NOTES

YOU MADE IT!

LET'S LOOK AT YOUR YEARLY WRAP-UP...

12 MONTH SUMMARY: INCOME STREAMS

Income Stream	Expected	Actual	Difference [+/-]	Notes
Total:				

12 MONTH SUMMARY: INCOME TOTALS

Month	Expected	Actual	Difference [+/-]	Notes
Total:				

12 MONTH SUMMARY: PERSONAL EXPENSES

Month	Category	Expected	Actual	Difference [+/-]	Notes
	Rent				
	Utilities				
	Transportation				
	Food				
	Entertainment				
	Health				
	Total:				

—12 MONTH SUMMARY: BUSINESS EXPENSES

Month	Category	Expected	Actual	Difference [+/-]	Notes
	Education				
	Marketing/Ads				
	Tech Equipment				
	Total:				

12 MONTH SUMMARY: PROFIT/LOSS

Month	Income	Expenses	Difference [+/-]	Notes
Total:				

Notes:

—AFTER-TAX INCOME

Once you've calculated your state and federal tax payments, then you can see your **net income—the money you earn that you get to keep**.

Calculate Net Income

	$	Gross (Total) Annual Income
-	$	Social Security Tax
-	$	Federal Income Tax
-	$	State Income Tax
=	$	Net Income

WRAP-UP REFLECTIONS

	Month	Amount	Notes
Lowest Month of Income			
Highest Month of Income			
Lowest Month of Personal Expenses			
Highest Month of Personal Expenses			
Lowest Month of Business Expenses			
Highest Month of Business Expenses			
Lowest Month of Long-term Planning			
Highest Month of Long-term Planning			

Notes:

WRAP-UP REFLECTIONS

What did I do well?

WRAP-UP REFLECTIONS

What did I struggle with?

WRAP-UP REFLECTIONS

How can I improve?

INTENTIONS FOR NEXT YEAR

As you're working on your yearly wrap-up, it's a good time to **start setting your intentions** for next year.

Build on what you've learned from tracking your money, and consider treating yourself to a fresh workbook to take your management skills to the next level in the new year.

RESOURCES + HELPFUL INFO

DISCLAIMER REMINDER:

This publication is intended to provide information based on the author's own experience and extensive research. However, it is **not intended to provide legal or financial advice**, nor should it be used as such without first consulting with a legal or financial professional to determine what is best for your individual needs. **The author and publisher specifically disclaim any liability, loss, or risk, personal or otherwise**, which may be incurred as a result of the use of this book.

– FINANCIAL TERMS YOU SHOULD KNOW

IRA

Individual retirement account.

- **Traditional IRA:**
  An account that allows you to set aside a limited amount of pretax money for a tax break now. Money in this account can't be accessed until you're 59.5 at the earliest. You will pay taxes when you withdraw.
- **Roth IRA:**
  An account that lets you set aside money after taxes so that it will be tax-free when it's withdrawn. Be aware, there are stricter limits for how much money you can put in a Roth IRA each year, and if you make more than a certain amount of income, you may not be eligible to use it at all.

Fiduciary

A person or organization that acts on behalf of another person or organization to manage assets.

Accountant (CPA)

A certified professional accountant is someone who has been trained to prepare financial documents such as profit-and-loss statements and balance sheets, prepare reports for tax purposes, and potentially even manage bookkeeping.

Bookkeeping

Records of a company's or person's financial transactions such as income and expenses.

Financial Advisor

A person who gives advice on the best strategies to achieve financial goals and helps with both short-term and long-term investments.

FINANCIAL TERMS YOU SHOULD KNOW

Money Market

A type of savings account that yields higher interest rates than a regular savings account, though it may have higher minimum deposit and balance requirements as well.

Certificate of Deposit (CD)

A forced savings account with an interest rate. These usually have a better return rate than a money market. The tradeoff is that your money (and the interest it earns) is locked in during the term of the CD (six months to several years, depending on how long you get the CD for). In case of ultimate emergency, you can access your principal, though it may mean you lose your interest.

Mutual Fund

A mutual fund is an investment vehicle that's a little simpler than buying individual stocks. (The trade-off, of course, is that you have less control over what you're investing in.) Mutual funds are predetermined pools of stocks and bonds that individuals can buy into as investors. The companies managing the mutual funds try to keep a profitable balance of stocks within each fund, but your return on investment is ultimately dependent on the managing company's success. There are many kinds of mutual funds available, so you can buy funds that align with your values (sustainable companies only, for example) or funds that are weighted according to your anticipated retirement year.

Stock (a.k.a. share)

An investment that represents an ownership share in a particular company.

HOW TO MANAGE DEBT

I frequently get asked **whether you should save money or pay off debt first**. You're responsible for yourself, and the answer depends on what makes the most sense for you! That said, here are **a few things to keep in mind**:

- **Consider the interest rate on your debt**: The higher it is, the faster you should try to pay it off. If the interest rate is low, you have more wiggle room.
- **Pay on time:** Making your minimum payments on time is really important. Late payments can rack up fees quickly and impact your credit score negatively.
- **Pay more than the minimum:** If you can't, that's okay. But if you can afford it, paying even just a few dollars more than the minimum every month can make a big difference toward knocking that debt down.
- **Don't go beyond your limits:** Try not to max out your credit card(s). This will not only create more stress for you, but it's also likely to screw up your credit score. Ideally, stay at least 30% under your limit.
- **Keep an eye on your credit score:** Checking your credit score regularly (once or twice a year) can help you catch any problems (such as identity theft) before they really make a mess of things. But only check through reputable sources, such as annualcreditreport.com.
- **Keep an eye on your debt details:** You don't want to underestimate (or overestimate) the amount of debt you have. Know your balances, limits, and debt holders so that the unknown doesn't make things worse. Keep an eye on what your debt is actually costing you. It's not just about the principal (the money that you borrowed to begin with), but the interest and fees too. If you're not careful, those can compound and make things bad fast.
- **Consider how you're using debt:** Are you building credit, keeping yourself afloat, or splurging on life upgrades?
- **Cut your interest rate to save money:** See if you can transfer your credit card balance to a card with a 0% promotional rate, or look into refinancing any loans you have.
- **Don't forget to save:** Even though it might be tempting to put all your disposable funds toward your debt, it's helpful to have a cash reserve that you can use during an emergency to prevent loading yourself up with more debt.

A NOTE ABOUT LONG-TERM PLANNING

- You can't save when you're focusing on surviving, so **don't beat yourself up** if you haven't saved much.

- **Start with the basics:** Build your emergency savings first, even if it's just a few dollars at a time.

- **Diversify your income streams** so that if one dries up or you need to take a break, you won't be reliant on work you don't want to (or can't) do.

- If you historically have a "see it, spend it" approach to your money, **open a savings account and set up an automatic deposit** so you won't see that money in your checking.

- **Use tools, services, and professionals that are designed to help you.** You don't have to rely on your will power, and you deserve to have support in reaching your goals.

- Ready to **think about investing?** Do your research, and get some help.

- In fact, **doing research and getting help are good guidelines to follow** in every aspect of your financial planning.

- It may seem counterintuitive, but you're often **better off buying a higher quality version of the items you need** rather than buying cheaper versions you'll have to replace frequently. You're likely to spend more money in the long run that way.

- **Make a plan!** Don't just "feel" your way toward your goal. Make a short-term plan and a long-term plan (5, 10, or 20 years).

- **Live beneath your means** in as many areas of your life as possible.

SUGGESTED READING

- ***Profit First: Transform Your Business from a Cash-Eating Monster to a Money-Making Machine***
  Mike Michalowicz

- ***You Are a Badass At Making Money: Master the Mindset of Wealth***
  By Jen Sincero

- ***Total Money Makeover: Classic Edition: a Proven Plan for Financial Fitness***
  Dave Ramsey

- ***Thriving in Sex Work: Sex Work and Money***
  Lola Davina

RECOMMENDED TOOLS

- **Mint** (app): A financial management tool that consolidates all of your accounts, bills, and credit information into one place.
  mint.com

- **You Need a Budget** (app): A budget and savings tool that's designed to help you feel in control of your money.
  youneedabudget.com

- **Qapital** (app): A banking and investing app that uses behavioral psychology to make saving easier.
  qapital.com

- **Quickbooks:** The classic business software has different pricing tiers to give flexibility depending on your needs.
  quickbooks.intuit.com

ABOUT THE AUTHOR

Princess Kali has **lived and breathed kink** both personally and professionally for twenty years, and she manages to embody two seemingly contradictory traits as a sexuality educator: **she is both tough love and enthusiastic cheerleader**. She understands the inherent fears, desires, and uncertainties that come with kink sexuality, and she spends a great deal of time **helping people become comfortable and confident** with pushing their boundaries.

Having witnessed similar fears, desires, and uncertainties around money and financial planning among her community of erotic professionals, **she's made it her mission to help her peers become as comfortable and confident** in the financial arena as they are in the sexual arena.

As the founder of **Erotication.com**, Kali is also a pioneer of the "kinktrepreneur" business model, creating sites such as **Kink Academy**, **Passionate U**, and **Fearless Press**, to provide the general public with easy access to adult sex and BDSM education. In 2020 she launched the **Red Key Club**, a business and marketing school for sex workers. Her work continues to inspire and support many other kink educators, writers, and enthusiasts.

OTHER BOOKS BY PRINCESS KALI

Sex + Kink

- *365 Days of Kink*
- *Authentic Kink*
- *Enough To Make You Blush: Exploring Erotic Humiliation*
- *Enough To Make You Blush: Companion Workbook*
- *The Yes, No, Maybe Workbook*
- *The ProDomme Playbook*
- *Red Umbrella Reflections*

Confidence + Empowerment

(Written under the name "Kali Williams")

- *Ditch the Bitch Stigma: Embrace Your Inner Badass*
- *Embrace Your Inner Badass: Companion Workbook*

ACKNOWLEDGEMENTS

This workbook has been the most unexpected project I've ever done. When I told my mom about it, she said "How great that after all the years of you feeling like money management wasn't something you could do, now you've created something that helps others," and I think that really sums up why I'm particularly proud.

Of course, **I didn't create this resource on my own**, so I want to share my very special thanks for the folks who helped me on my own financial journey, and those that brought this workbook into reality.

My first thanks go to Marcia and Zed and all the money talks, business brainstorming, and mutual cheerleading sessions that have been such a big part of my personal and professional growth.

Thank you to all of the Red Key Club members who have inspired me so much this year. You are all brilliant, badass entrepreneurs who overcome gigantic mountains of obstacles to run a business that you're proud of and that the world needs. Your feedback, support, and camaraderie mean the world to me.

Big thanks to my fabulous friend Vivienne Kramer, who joined us at the RKC for monthly money management discussions. You helped create an accessible space for everyone (including me!) based on the "there's no question too dumb" rule, and I'm so deeply grateful to you for sharing your expertise with us. And bonus thanks for all the feedback on this workbook!

My thanks also goes to Holly GoLightly, one of the most engaged and enthusiastic members of the Red Key Club. Your thorough and constructive feedback has been incredibly handy in helping me refine my classes and this workbook.

My continued gratitude goes to my graphic designer Hannah Portello-Swagel for creating yet another bold cover and dynamic layout. You're always a delight to work with!

Lastly, thank you to Sarah Welch for being such a whip-sharp editor and for helping me improve this project and every other project you help me with!

Made in United States
North Haven, CT
21 October 2026

20740134R00128